A+
books

A Day in the Life of a
CHIPMUNK
A 4D BOOK

by Sharon Katz Cooper

Consultant: Robert T. Mason
Professor of Integrative Biology
J.C. Braly Curator of Vertebrates
Oregon State University

PEBBLE
a capstone imprint

Download the Capstone 4D app!

- Ask an adult to download the Capstone 4D app.
- Scan the cover and stars inside the book for additional content.

When you scan a spread, you'll find fun extra stuff to go with this book! You can also find these things on the web at www.capstone4D.com using the password: chipmunk.15152

A+ Books are published by Pebble
1710 Roe Crest Drive, North Mankato, Minnesota 56003
www.mycapstone.com

Library of Congress Cataloging-in-Publication Data
Names: Katz Cooper, Sharon, author.
Title: A day in the life of a chipmunk : a 4D book / by Shannon Katz Cooper.
Description: North Mankato, Minnesota : an imprint of Pebble, [2019] |
   Series: A+ books. A day in the life | Audience: Age 4–8.
Identifiers: LCCN 2018006120 (print) | LCCN 2018009142 (ebook) |
   ISBN 9781543515237 (eBook PDF) | ISBN 9781543515152 (library binding) |
   ISBN 9781543515190 (paperback)
Subjects: LCSH: Chipmunks—Life cycles—Juvenile literature.
Classification: LCC QL737.R68 (ebook) | LCC QL737.R68 K38 2019 (print) |
   DDC 599.36/4—dc23
LC record available at https://lccn.loc.gov/2018006120

Editorial Credits
Gina Kammer, editor; Jennifer Bergstrom, designer;
Morgan Walters, media researcher; Laura Manthe, production specialist

Photo Credits
Getty Images: Alina Morozova, 24, Don Johnston, 22, Frank Cezus, 5, STEVE MASLOWSKI, 26, TOM MCHUGH, 16;, Virginia P Weinland, 25; Minden Pictures: S and D and K Maslowski, 27; Shutterstock: Breck P. Kent, 12, 29, Brian Lasenby, 18, colacat, 7, David Havel, 9, dugdax, 4, Fiona M. Donnelly, 19, IRA_EVVA, 11, Kris Wiktor, 17, Lizov Ivan, 6, Margaret M Stewart, 15, Mircea Costina, 1, Orfeev, Cover, design element throughout, Paul Reeves Photography, 21, 30, Ron Rowan Photography, 23, Stastny_Pavel, 8, Svetlana Foote, 20, Valerii Shkliaev, Cover, William G Carpenter, 13

Note to Parents, Teachers, and Librarians

This book uses full color photographs and a nonfiction format to introduce the concept of a chipmunk's day. *A Day in the Life of a Chipmunk* is designed to be read aloud to a pre-reader or to be read independently by an early reader. Photographs help listeners and early readers understand the text and concepts discussed. The book encourages further learning by including the following sections: Table of Contents, Glossary, Read More, Internet Sites, Critical Thinking Questions, and Index. Early readers may need assistance using these features.

Printed in the United States of America.
PA017

TABLE OF CONTENTS

A Chipmunk's Day

Inside her burrow, the chipmunk opens her eyes. She uncurls her tail from her small furry body. Her paws stretch out. She runs down a long tunnel and pokes her head outside.

There's the sun! It peeks out through the trees. The morning is warm in the forest. The chipmunk has a busy day ahead.

The chipmunk darts out of her hole in the ground. She looks for nuts, seeds, and berries to eat.

MUNCH!

She also looks for small bugs. She stuffs them inside her cheeks.

All morning, the chipmunk runs through the forest. She also listens and watches. For what? She watches for predators. Hawks, foxes, and snakes eat chipmunks! She's a perfect snack for them. She's 9 inches (23 centimeters) long and weighs 3 ounces (85 grams). She could fit inside a cereal bowl!

HIDE!

When her cheeks are full, the chipmunk runs to her burrow. The burrow has many tunnels. Some have space to store food. There's lots to eat in the forest now. But in winter, there won't be much. The chipmunk stores food for later.

The chipmunk does not hibernate all winter like some other mammals. Instead, she will be dormant. She will sleep almost all day. When she gets hungry, she will wake up and eat a little.

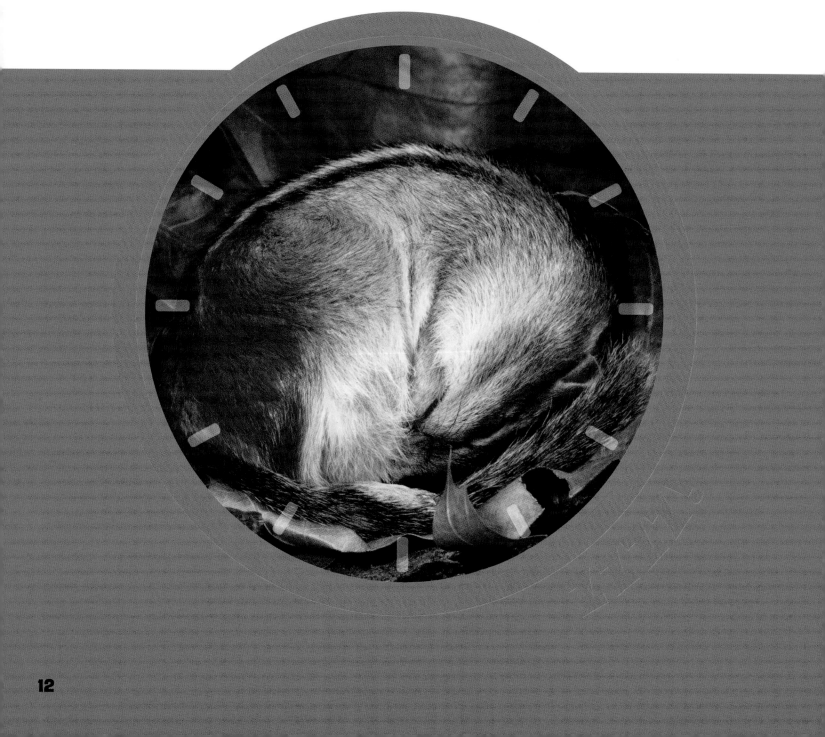

Her stored food has to last all winter. She has to pile it up in the summer and fall.

Today the chipmunk has something else to do too. She has four new babies! They are called pups. The pups are tiny. They can't yet feed themselves. The chipmunk feeds her pups milk from her body.

The pups will stay with their mother for two months. Then, they will have to learn to find food on their own.

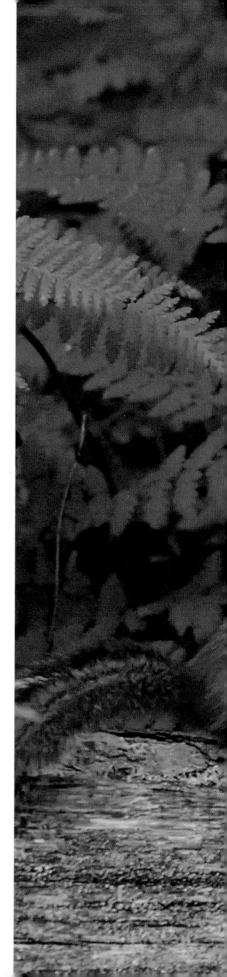

The chipmunk's pups are the size of bumblebees when they are born. They cannot see. They have no hair. They start to get their stripy fur after eight days.

The chipmunk takes care of her pups by herself. She feeds and protects them. She also protects the opening to her burrow.

What's that? The chipmunk sees another chipmunk nearby! She makes a loud chirping sound. *CHK, CHK!* It's a warning to stay away!

The chipmunk runs into the forest again in the afternoon. She climbs and jumps from branch to branch. She sniffs under leaves and logs. She looks for more food.

SNIFF!

When she hears or sees danger, she stops
to hide. Her reddish-brown color hides her
in the leaves.

CUK-CUK-CUK. CUK-CUK-CUK. CHIRP CHIRP.
The chipmunk stops to listen. The calls warn her
of danger. Or maybe she is stepping in another
chipmunk's territory. Chipmunks talk a lot!

CUK-CUK!

The sun sets. The chipmunk runs home to her burrow.

RUN!

She re-uses tunnels dug by other animals for her burrow. Or sometimes she widens tunnels made by tree roots. That's easier than digging tunnels all on her own.

By the end of fall, the chipmunk's burrow will hold as many as 5,000 to 6,000 nuts. She needs lots of space. Her many tunnels give her room for food.

They also have room for sleeping and places to
hide her pups. She uses her strong front legs to dig
a tunnel out a little longer. There! More space!

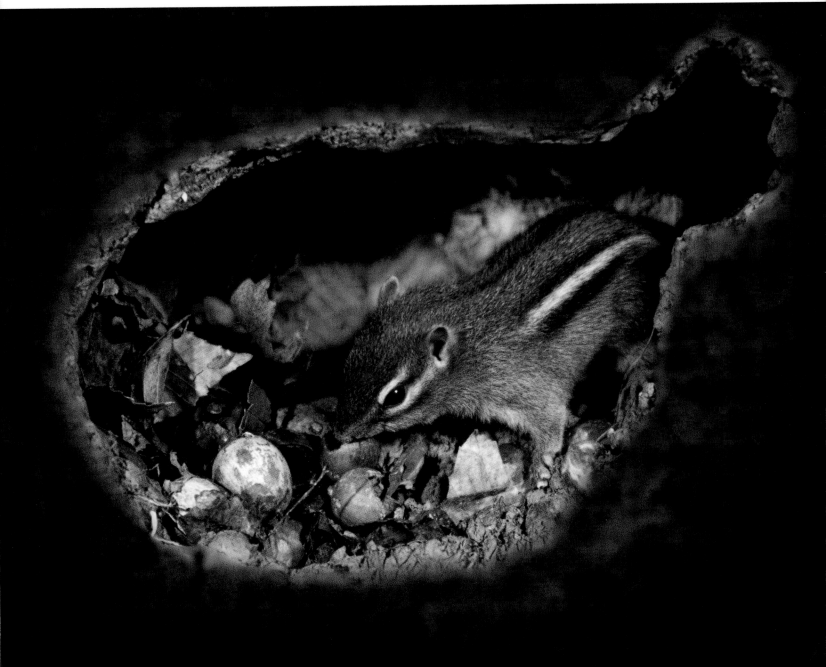

It grows dark in the forest. The day ends. The chipmunk curls around her pups. She feeds them again and closes her eyes. Time to get some rest for the next busy day.

Good night, chipmunk!

LIFE CYCLE OF A CHIPMUNK

1 Between **FEBRUARY** and **APRIL** each year, chipmunks mate.

2 The mother chipmunk is pregnant for about **31 DAYS.**

3 Chipmunks begin life as tiny **BEE-SIZED** pups. They are hairless, and their eyes are closed.

4 After about **4 WEEKS,** the pups go out of their burrows to find their own food.

5 After **6** to **8 WEEKS,** the pups live on their own.

6 After **ONE YEAR,** the grown chipmunks have their own pups.

Glossary

burrow—a hole in the ground made or used by an animal

dormant—not active

hibernate—to spend winter in a deep sleep

mammal—a warm-blooded animal that breathes air; mammals have hair or fur; female mammals feed milk to their young

mate—to join together to produce young

predator—an animal that hunts other animals for food

protect—to keep safe

territory—an area of land defended by an animal or group of animals

warn—to tell about a danger that might happen in the future

Read More

Gregory, Josh. *Chipmunks*. Nature's Children. New York: Children's Press, 2015.

Schuh, Mari. *Chipmunks*. Backyard Animals. North Mankato, Minn: Capstone Press, 2015.

Strattin, Lisa. *Facts About Chipmunks: A Picture Book for Kids*. Facts for Kids Picture Books, Volume 5. CreateSpace Independent Publishing Platform, 2015.

Internet Sites

Use FactHound to find Internet sites related to this book.

Visit *www.facthound.com*

Just type in 9781543515152 and go.

Check out projects, games and lots more at
www.capstonekids.com

Critical Thinking Questions

1. Why do you think a chipmunk would re-use tunnels built by other animals?

2. Why do chipmunks work so hard to collect food during the fall?

3. How do chipmunk pups look different from their mothers?

Index